FEBRUARY 2011

To WENDY ON HER BIRTHDAY.
PUBLISHED THE YEAR IT
ALL (RE)-STARTED — FOR ME
... + YOU. WE ALL MUST HAVE
FAITH IN SOMETHING.

I IN YOU.

YOURS, C

SINNERS WELCOME

ALSO BY MARY KARR

Cherry

Viper Rum

The Liars' Club

The Devil's Tour

Abacus

HarperCollins*Publishers*

SINNERS
WELCOME

POEMS

MARY KARR

HarperCollins books may be purchased for educational, business, or sales promotional use. For information, please write: Special Markets Department, HarperCollins Publishers, 10 East 53rd Street, New York, NY 10022.

FIRST EDITION

Designed by Lucy Albanese

Printed on acid-free paper

Library of Congress Cataloging-in-Publication Data

Karr, Mary.
Sinners welcome : poems/Mary Karr.
p.   cm.
ISBN-10: 0-06-077654-4
ISBN-13: 978-0-06-077654-1
I. Title.

PS3561.A6929S57   2006
813'.54—dc22   2005050328

06   07   08   09   10   ❖ / RRD   10   9   8   7   6   5   4   3   2   1

FOR MY SISTER, LECIA SCAGLIONE

whose larger hand steered mine
around that first, tortured cursive.
Earliest reader, queen of the straight shot
and the crossword, you're the one
I've always scribbled toward.

ACKNOWLEDGMENTS

Ongoing gratitude to Brooks Haxton for his example, his hatchet, and his pool shark's eye.

My editor, Courtney Hodell, never fails at trim and gusset, cross-stich or love knot.

Robert Hass, Brenda Hillman, Edward Hirsch, and Stuart Dybek all tried to keep my butcher's thumb off the scale. Rodney Crowell and Awadagin Pratt provided the music.

Thanks to Dean Catherine Newton and William Safire for helping to carve a home for me at Syracuse University's College of Arts and Sciences. The John Simon Guggenheim Memorial Foundation also funded me after eighteen applications.

Some of these poems appeared in the following newspapers or magazines:

The New Yorker: "Pathetic Fallacy," "The Choice," "Orphanage," "A Blessing from My Sixteen Years' Son," "Last Love," "Still Memory," "Hurt Hospital's Best Suicide Jokes."

The Atlantic Monthly: "Sinners Welcome," "Who the Meek Are Not," "Meditatio."

Poetry: "Métaphysique du Mal," "Revelations in the Key of K," "A Tapestry Figure Escapes for Occupancy in the Real World, Which Includes the Death of Her Mother," "Disgraceland." From the *Descending Theology* series: "Christ Human," "The Resurrection."

Parnassus: "A Major." From the *Descending Theology* series: "The Nativity," "The Crucifixion," "Coat Hanger Bent into Halo," "Reference for Ex-Man's Next."

Ploughshares: "Elegy for a Rain Salesman."

The Kenyon Review: "This Lesson You've Got," "Requiem."

Cincinnati Review: "For a Dying Tomcat Who's Abandoned His Former Hissing and Predatory Nature."

Corresponding Voices: "The Ice Fisherman," "Pluck," "Winter Term's End," "The First Step."

Best American Poetry 2005: "A Blessing from My Sixteen Years' Son."

Washington Post Book World: "Descending Theology: The Crucifixion."

The Paris Review: "Delinquent Missive," "Miss Flame, Apartment Bound, as Undiscovered Porn Star."

Other anthologies also ran poems: *The Poet's Choice, Sweet Jesus, The Norton Introduction to Poetry.* Some poems were anthologized on radio cassettes and CDs: Garrison Keillor's *Prairie Home Companion,* National Public Radio's *Fresh Air,* and *All Things Considered.*

For spiritual aid and sacred hilarity, Patti Macmillan's hand has been on my shoulder thirteen lucky years. My other Virgil was Paul Stephen Goggi, Jr. My physical trainer was Steve Friedman.

Also my presumed thesis students, Sarah Harwell and Courtney Queeney, taught me way more than I did them. Praise them and their sister Laments for crucial instruction in lake-effect weeping.

. . . And I waited with anxious soul for Romeo to descend from the clouds, a satin Romeo singing of love, while backstage a dejected electrician waits with his finger on the button to turn off the moon.

—ISAAC BABEL, *Red Cavalry*

《 《 《

God says, to the free mind, *Find me.*

—BROOKS HAXTON "Anonymous"
Nakedness, Death, and the Number Zero

CONTENTS

SINNERS WELCOME

PATHETIC FALLACY

When it became impossible to speak to you
due to your having died and been incinerated,
I sometimes held the uncradled phone

with its neat digits and arcane symbols (crosshatch,
black star) as if embedded in it
were some code I could punch in

to reach you. You bequeathed me
this morbid bent, Mother.
Who gives her sixth-grade daughter

Sartre's *Nausea* to read? All my life,
I watched you face the void,
leaning into it as a child with a black balloon

will bury her countenance
either to hide from
or to merge with that darkness.

Small wonder that still
in the invisible scrim of air
that delineates our separate worlds,

your features sometimes press toward me
all silvery from the afterlife, woven in wind,
to whisper a caution. Or your hand on my back

shoves me into my life.

REVELATIONS IN THE KEY OF K

I came awake in kindergarten,
under the letter K chalked neat
on a field-green placard leaned

on the blackboard's top edge. They'd caged me
in a metal *desk*—the dull word writ
to show K's sound. But K meant *kick* and *kill*

when a boy I'd kissed drew me
as a whiskered troll in art. On my sheet,
the puffy clouds I made to keep rain in

let torrents dagger loose. "Screw those
who color in the lines," my mom had preached,
words I shared that landed me on a short chair

facing the corner's empty Sheetrock page. Craning up,
I found my K high above.
You'll have to grow to here, its silence said.

And in the surrounding alphabet, my whole life hid—
names of my beloveds, sacred vows I'd break.
With my pencil stub applied to wall,

I moved around the loops and vectors,
Z to A, learning how to mean, how
in the mean world to be.

But while I worked, the room around me
began to smudge—like a charcoal sketch my mom
was rubbing with her thumb. Then

the instant went, the month, and every season
smeared, till with a wrenching arm tug
I was here, grown, but still bent

to set down words before the black eraser
swipes our moment into cloud, dispersing all
to zip. And when I blunder in the valley

of the shadow of blank about to break
in half, my being leans against my spinal K,
which props me up, broomstick straight,

a strong bone in the crypt of flesh I am.

ORATORIO FOR THE UNBECOMING

Born, I eventually grew hind legs
to rear back on, and learned I was other
than the miasma that mothered me,
so begged to reenter the body. Told no,
I staggered forth to whap my head on table corners—
my tongue a small stub jabbering wants.

In the morning funnies, Little Orphan Annie
had an eye like a white pindot,
and when I watched her blankly
watching me, the complex universe
crawled inside my head.
Mirrors spooked me too. The kid inside

eluded me, though her fingertips
fit perfectly to mine. The mystery of who she was
floated on a silver surface uncertain as mercury.
The heart is a mirror also, and in my chest I felt
this tight bud of petals held a face:
God, with his stare of a zillion suns.

He told me the risen Lord was a sack of meat
and a brother to me, that the Holy Ghost
was the girl pronoun in sacred texts
who longed to steer
my body's ship. He swears now

this form is carved by him.
Have mercy, the soul
singer says, and I say
blessed be the air
I breathe these words with, for

it makes a body wonder.

Before my first communion at 40, I clung
    to doubt as Satan spider-like stalked
        the orb of dark surrounding Eden
            for a wormhole into paradise.

God had first formed me in the womb
    small as a bite of burger.
        Once my lungs were done
            He sailed a soul like a lit arrow

to inflame me. Maybe that piercing
    made me howl at birth,
        or the masked creatures
            whose scalpel cut a lightning bolt to free me—

I was hoisted by the heels and swatted, fed
    and hauled through rooms. Time-lapse photos show
        my fingers grew past crayon outlines,
            my feet came to fill spike heels.

Eventually, I lurched out to kiss the wrong mouths,
    get stewed, and sulk around. Christ always stood
        to one side with a glass of water.
        I swatted the sap away.

When my thirst got great enough
    to ask, a stream welled up inside;
        some jade wave buoyed me forward;
        and I found myself upright

in the instant, with a garden
    inside my own ribs aflourish. There, the arbor leafs.
        The vines push out plump grapes.
            You are loved, someone said. Take that

and eat it.

MÉTAPHYSIQUE DU MAL

Sometimes in the quadrangled globe you feel
impossibly small, a mere pushpin with face
embossed on top, jabbed in place.

Say it's night in the kitchen, and those sprawled pages
hold notes for your oldest friend's funeral—your fifth
eulogy in five years. Bach's
measuring out cool intervals of pain.

You stand too long in the freezerspill
of smoky Arctic twilight—rows of plastic boxes
old soups and gravies
furred with frost, everything glazed in place.
And in the fridge, how long has that stripped carcass
shriveled there, legs widespread?
In the pantry, the lychee nuts eyeball you,
aloof in their ancient miasma of syrup.

By dawn, pantries yawn on all sides. Bach's shut off.
Every dog-eared tome has been thumbed.
The single page says only, I had a friend who died. Cancer
ate her liver out. In your Timex

the noise shifts, the minuscule hammers
start tapping out *now, now* abruptly fast.

(for Patti Mora)

DESCENDING THEOLOGY: THE NATIVITY

She bore no more than other women bore,
but in her belly's globe that desert night the earth's
full burden swayed.
Maybe she held it in her clasped hands as expecting women often do
or monks in prayer. Maybe at the womb's first clutch
      she briefly felt that star shine

as a blade point, but uttered no curses.
Then in the stable she writhed and heard
beasts stomp in their stalls,
their tails sweeping side to side
and between contractions, her skin flinched
with the thousand animal itches that plague
      a standing beast's sleep.

But in the muted womb-world with its glutinous liquid,
the child knew nothing
of its own fire. (No one ever does, though our names
are said to be writ down before
we come to be.) He came out a sticky grub, flailing
      the load of his own limbs

and was bound in cloth, his cheek brushed
with fingertip touch
so his lolling head lurched, and the sloppy mouth
found that first fullness—her milk
spilled along his throat, while his pure being
      flooded her. (Each

feeds the other.) Then he was left
in the grain bin. Some animal muzzle
against his swaddling perhaps breathed him warm
till sleep came pouring that first draught
of death, the one he'd wake from
        (as we all do) screaming.

Before David Ricardo stabbed his daddy
      sixteen times with a fork—*Once*
for every year of my fuckwad life—he'd long
     showed signs of being bent.
In school, he got no valentine nor birthday
      cake embellished with his name.
On Halloween, a towel tied around his neck
      was all he had to be a hero with.
He spat in the punchbowl and smelled like a foot.
      His forehead was a ledge
he leered beneath. When I was sent to tutor him
      in geometry, so he might leave
(at last) ninth grade, he sat running pencil lead
      beneath his nails.
If radiance shone from those mudhole eyes,
      I missed it. Thanks, David
for your fine slang. You called my postulates
      post holes; your mom endured
ferocious of the liver. Plus you ignored—
      when I saw you wave at lunch—
my flinch. Maybe by now you're ectoplasm,
      or the zillionth winner of the Texas
death penalty sweepstakes. Or you occupy
      a locked room with a small
round window held fast by rivets, through which
      you are watched. But I hope
some organism drew your care—orchid
      or cockroach even, some inmate

in a wheelchair whose steak you had to cut
        since he lacked hands.
In this way, the unbudgeable stone
        that plugged the tomb hole
in your chest could roll back, and in your sad
        slit eyes could blaze
that star adored by its maker.

THIS LESSON YOU'VE GOT

to learn is the someday you'll someday
stagger to, blinking in cold light, all tears
shed, ready to poke your bovine head
      in the yoke they've shaped.

Everyone learns this. Born, everyone
breathes, pays tax, plants dead
and hurts galore. There's grief enough
      for each. My mother

learned by moving man to man,
outlived them all. The parched earth's
bare (once she leaves it) of any who watched
      the instants I trod it.

Other than myself, of course.
I've made a study of bearing
and forbearance. Everyone does,
      it turns out, and note

those faces passing by: Not one's a god.

THE CHOICE

Once in northern England, I got a few pub drunks
to drive to Wordsworth's house, local thugs
whose underheated VW (orange) took me
fishtailing down icy hills,

through hedgerows in an unlit labyrinth
reminiscent of the library stacks I wandered around
zombie-like each day, not composing
verses but waiting in scarlet lipstick

for the bars to open. I'd left my homeland
fleeing a man I'd faked first caring, then
not caring about, and in months of Euclidean solitude
I'd writ no cogent phrase. The notebook in my knapsack

was a talisman I carried into train stations so as not
to look like a bimbo. But bimbo
I was, and open, the bound pages were only white wings
to nap on. Near dawn, our caravan came

to a sleet-glazed window—a child's stumpy desk
with the poet's initials penknifed on top.
It was my first stab of reverence,
when that hunger to emblazon

some surface with oneself became barbarous
wonder at someone else. *W.W.*—
jagged as inverted Alps, unscalable
as a cathedral's gold-leaf dome.

After that, grad school was a must.
There I posed as supplicant till enough
magnificence had been poured
down my throat that I could whiff

the difference between it and the stench
I spilled. When I told the resident genius
that given the choice between writing and being
happy, I'd pick the latter, she touched my folio

with her pencil like a bad fairy's wand,
saying: *Don't worry, you don't have that choice.*
And in a blink of my un-mascara'ed eye
the intricate world bloomed into being—impossible

to transcribe on the small bare page.

(for Brooks Haxton)

A MAJOR

I've come to see a dread-locked man
play Mozart like a demon (someone said) with angels
harrowing his back, or like a seraph
sought by succubi.
The black piano waits wide-legged, in boxer's pose.
It's a sarcophagus that stores

whole flocks of birds, banks of cirrus clouds,
Egyptian forest groves,
and a thousand metaphysical motes
to sting a watcher's eyes like sleet.
A corps in funeral dress lines up in rows,
but the piano holds the most tonight.

We gather on its rim and hunger towards it,
till the stage man props its jaw wide.
Then out strides this lion-headed man,
whom everyone can see the weather in. Then
the winds inhale, and the bows tilt at even angles
like the tiny masts of lifted sails.

Right away, the piano's notes unknot
some inner ropes in me, hoist some mainsheet,
loose in us some breeze, and with a broad wave
of the maestro's wand, we're off,
the notes skittering us along
like surf. The keys are black and bone and pose

a hurried order. When his lion's head
drops back, his face becomes a soft-edged mask
lifted in defiance of the night we came here
stalled in. See, my face is wet
I never haven't breathed so long. I've seen
a death with order, meant but no way mean.

He's sprung our sternums wide
and freed us from our numbered seats.
We levitate as one and try to match
the thunder in his chest
with all our hands.

(for Awadagin Pratt)

WAITING FOR GOD: SELF-PORTRAIT AS SKELETON

Need is a death's head —SIMONE WEIL

The winter Mother's ashes came in a Ziploc bag,
all skin was scorched from me, and my skull
was a hard helmet I wore to pray
with my middle finger bone aimed at the light fixture—*Come out,
You fuck,* I'd say, then wait for God to finish me
where I knelt; or for my dead mother to assemble in clouds
of the Aquanet hairspray she'd used abundantly
in her bleach blond *Flashdance* phase at sixty when she'd phone
all slurry and sequined with disco playing to weep
so I'd send cash, and once she splurged on a bloated sofa
and matching Lazy-Boy recliner where her fat love could sprawl
with gold chains on his hairy chest while she painted the mural
of hippos to honor their nude abundances. Was it God
who dragged her from the kitchen floor
where she'd puked and the guy had pissed himself
to detox, to a rickety chair where she eventually sat upright
with eyes clear as seawater? *Yes,* I said
to myself one day, kneeling, *I believe
that's right.* Then from the hard knot at my skull's base
I felt warm oil as from a bath bead broken open
somehow flow upward to cover my skull, and my hair
came streaming down again,
and the soft clay crawled back to form my face.

(for Kent Scott)

AT THE SOUND OF THE GUNSHOT,
LEAVE A MESSAGE

That's what my friend spoke
into his grim machine the winter he first went mad
as we both did in our thirties with still
no hope of revenue, gravely inking
our poems on pages held fast by gyres
          the color of lead.

Godless, our minds
did monster us, left us bobbing as in a swamp
until we sank. His eyes were burn holes
in a swollen face. His breath was a venom
he drank deep of. He called his own tongue
          a scar, this poet

who can crowbar open
the most sealed heart, make ash flower,
and the cocked shotgun's double-zero mouths
(whose pellets had exploded star holes into plaster and porcelain
and not a few locked doors) never touched
          my friend's throat. Praise

Him, whose earth is green.

(for Franz Wright)

ELEGY FOR A RAIN SALESMAN

Dear friend, I heard tonight by phone
of that ghost bubble in your brain.
It was not the pearl of balance one fits
between lines in a carpenter's level
to make something plumb, but a blip
in a membrane that burst so now
       your fine brain is dead—

that city of mist that nests in your skull
will never again flicker with light.
Flying the red-eye home, I talked to your mom tonight
by air phone. Through static
her voice stayed calm, wondering when
to unhook the hospital's bellows.
       She thought a trip

to the beauty shop would help, and John,
how you'd have cackled at that.
That winter when I was broke
and camped on your sofa for months,
your dusky laugh kept me alive.
Each night in a menthol fog we drank
       till last call.

Once staggering home, we stopped
to crane up between buildings, lines of windows
rising away in rows. We listed in wonder,
leaning together like cartoon drunks. There was

a rectangle of sparkled sky you pointed out—
beauty's tattered flag—we pledged allegiance to—
        mittens over our heaving chests,

cold to break your teeth on,
a jillion stars foretelling none of this. Your mom said
your last sight on earth was your own face
in the shaving glass—in that hermit's flat on Colfax Ave.
where I watched you tape to the bathroom wall
the first *New Yorker* rejection of hundreds.

        So that monocled asshole
on the letterhead must have recurred
like wallpaper four hundred times
behind your moon face rising. Freeze
that frame. Let me hold awhile
with imagined hands that face,
as you might have briefly held that day
        the worn oval of soap,

        idly, with no thought of its vanishing.
Let me watch you shape in your palm
a frail Everest of shaving foam,
then smear yourself a snowman's face
with coal eyes staring out. The night
that drew our drunk salute has now
        bled into that skull,

glazed its porcelain with spider cracks
like a Grecian urn. Our time's
run out, no epitaph on which to land safe
appears in my oval porthole. The prairie slides beneath
me white as any page. And rain has hardened
into ticking sleet. Sleep, friend, as I cannot, reading
        the lines you left,

streaking behind you like a meteor trail:

        . . . . *I wanted to be a rain salesman,*
carrying my satchel full of rain from door to door,
selling thunder, selling the way air feels after a downpour,
but there are no openings in the rain department,
and so they left me dying behind this desk—adding bleeps,
subtracting chunks—and I would give a bowl of wild blossoms,
some rain, and two shakes of my fist at the sky to be living. . . .

                    (for John Engman, 1949–1996)

WHO THE MEEK ARE NOT

Not the bristle-bearded Igors bent
under burlap sacks, not peasants knee-deep
    in the rice paddy muck,
nor the serfs whose quarter-moon sickles
    make the wheat fall in waves
they don't get to eat. My friend the Franciscan
    nun says we misread
that word *meek* in the Bible verse that blesses them.
    To understand the meek
(she says) picture a great stallion at full gallop
    in a meadow, who—
at his master's voice—seizes up to a stunned
    but instant halt.
So with the strain of holding that great power
    in check, the muscles
along the arched neck keep eddying,
    and only the velvet ears
prick forward, awaiting the next order.

HYPERTROPHIED FOOTBALL STAR
AS SERIAL KILLER

1. *Double Sessions*

Sometimes the coach whapped his earhole;
or many linemen bulldozed his form
like a training sled, face mask turning up sod

for yards. When his brain bounced hard enough
the lights snapped out, and he was sidelined.
Still, if the whistle reached his sleeping ears, he'd bolt

from stretcher to green field helmetless.
Put me in, he'd say. That's heart,
said the coach, for whom a hit meant love.

2. *Romancing the Skull*

In bed, our football star spoke wordless rain
till a cool moon burned in a lady's pelvic lake.
Then he was ape again, the bringer

of bruises with an icepick stare.
He loved his women drugged enough
to pin like bugs, and found one starved:

picture a death's head in a velvet cape,
the only one he didn't kill, since she came
dead already. His face would bear the scars

her talons clawed the night he threw her out,
and she cut her wrist with an oiled and scented blade,
so the slit might exude rose attar

and not the stink of graves.

3.   *Keening, Nascent Time*

For weeks, he'd boil the skull, row it
to his private island, swing it from a tree limb
with other skulls above his hammock.

When he ran wind sprints in surf,
to feint and dodge his ghost opponents,
he felt the black eyeholes watching.

His own hair began to shed like leaves,
and his chest was snow, and winter
ran his face, and though he scrubbed himself

with mint, he could not clean the death off.
One night he knelt between
the legs of one he'd unrolled

all his ones for, and begged, *Put it in,* but softness
kept him out. He did her quick and left her head
attached, then rowed home bald and small.

4. *Pathos Unbound*

After the dropped oars came the island hours
when the mother tempest spun inside his head,
and he strapped on pads to charge at phantoms

bursting into spray, and bashed his face mask
till the mouth guard bent, but could not kill
the girl in him. He ended limping into slosh,

which ruffled his crotch in its yellowed cup.
The first wave to slap his chest made him
a babe again in water wings, paddling toward

the dwindling V of his father's arms.
Through darkening jade, he fell
weightless, as if bounding from the end zone

to catch a ball. It's said
when the mystery finally speaks,
you hear the void you've spoken

every longing into, silence articulate.
From his helmet's dead earphone
the words: *Just go out long, I'll find you.*

ORDERS FROM THE INVISIBLE

Insert coin. Mind the gap. Do not disturb
hung from the doorknob of a hotel room,
where a man begged to die entwined in my arms.

He once wrote
he'd take the third rail in his teeth, which is how
loving him turned out.
The airport's glass world
glided me gone from him, and the sky I flew into
grew a pearly cataract through which God
lost sight of us. *The moving walk*

is nearing its end.

The diner jukebox says, *Choose*
again, and the waitress hollers over,
"All them soul songs got broke."
She speaks from the cook's window, steam
smearing her face of all feature.

The tongue is a form of fire, the Bible says,
and in the computer's unstarred blue
the man's brutal missives
drag me along by my throat.

Press yes to erase.

REQUIEM: PROFESSOR WALT MINK (1927–1996)

My friend's eyelids were closed
with these thumbs, which left
faint whirlpools of skin oil.
It's okay. He'd stopped
seeing: The lifelong film unreeling behind his gaze
had stopped (sprocket jam, gear freeze, dim

to black). So the last frame burned out
(as I picture it) white on the brain's bulb.
No one could fix it, though this friend was a scientist,
and I'd watched his hands repair
the skull circuits of mice small as my thumb.
That was in my youth and in his tutelage.

And everyone he touched
seemed changed by it—brighter, faster, more
capable of love. Thinking of him
I feel pliable again.
I long for hands imbued
with grace to shape me.

And I worry the form I'll finally take (death
lesson) and whether I can be made to leave
on anyone some mark worth bearing.

PLUCK

That spring snow fell late and long to clog
every road away from the house my marriage
had withered in
and whose mortgage
I could scarce afford. Because my son

was young and my academic check
went poof each month
about day ten,
I developed pluck—
a trait much praised in Puritan texts,

which favor the spiritual clarity
suffering brings.
Pluck also keeps the low-cost, high-producing poor
digging post holes or loading deep-fat fryers
or holding tag sales where their poor

peers come to haggle over silver pie-slicers
once boxed special for a bride. This
wasn't real
poverty in America, but it soured my shrunk soul
to its nub. Nights, I lay on my mattress

on the floor, studying the clock face
with its flipping digits. One day I woke to sun
Then grass pushed up,
and my son trapped dozens of crickets
in a pickle jar's sharp, upended air.

In an old aquarium, he laid a shaggy carpet
of clover, apple hunks, and a mustard lid filled
with water—
covered with a screen, weighed
with the dictionary so the cats couldn't get in.

On Mothering Sunday, when one is obliged
to revere whatever bitch brought one
to this hard world,
my son led me down to a room
where crickets sang as if I were the sun.

Which I was, I guess, to him,
and him to me. After that, when a creditor rang
to bark his threats,
I set the phone down on the counter
so he could hear the crude creatures plucked

from the weeds by the boy, and what they sang.

DESCENDING THEOLOGY: CHRIST HUMAN

Such a short voyage for a god,
and you arrived in animal form so as not
to scorch us with your glory.
Your mask was an infant's head on a limp stalk,
sticky eyes smeared blind,
limbs rendered useless in swaddle.
You came among beasts
as one, came into our care or its lack, came crying
as we all do, because the human frame
is a crucifix, each skeletos borne a lifetime.
Any wanting soul lain
prostrate on a floor to receive a pouring of sunlight
might—if still enough,
feel your cross buried in the flesh.
One has only to surrender,
you preached, open both arms to the inner,
the ever-present hold,
out-reaching every want. It's in the form
embedded, love adamant as bone.
In a breath, we can bloom and almost be you

(for Paul Goggi)

MISS FLAME, APARTMENT BOUND,
AS UNDISCOVERED PORN STAR

Here in my lonely bed one day, I sprawled in silks.
There was a fire escape but no flame. Outside,
a world of brick. Through the sweatshop window
across the way, a man's face popped up, as if to study
my stalled lust. His stay was brief. Another face.
The men were taking turns—did they vie and jostle
for the briefest sight of me? Should I take myself in hand
and writhe? (On the net, I'd seen for sale The Little Minx
Stripper Pole. For a hundred bucks, I could buy a stake
for my gyrations, and show these strangers how an American slut
unwinds.) But it was day. The whole sun fell between us, filled
the alley: My windows were a total blank,

which was what my last lover saw—a brick himself.
Like him, the men were blind to me, taking turns at the pissoir.

REFERENCE FOR EX-MAN'S NEXT

after Catullus

When you climb the next lady's steps
     with your frat boy bounce, fist
gripped around some peonies, fresh steaming dough
     baked on your homely stone for her
alone, she should know that vows you spout
     would fill a stadium empty
as your chest; that the good emails you sent
     to grease her up ("'twas but a dream
of thee" and that ripe crap) were writ by Donne
     and meant no more than worms
you'd feed a stupid fish; that the hot girl slang
     you'll naked whisper came
from Bambi (sexysluts.com) and has been pitched
     as underhand and low to schoolgirls
you did con to bed—and yes, to me: dumb cunt.

The student pokes her head into my cubicle.
She's climbed the screw-thread stairs that spiral up
to the crow's nest where I work
to say goodbye.
She hands back books I lent.
I wave her to move papers from the spot

she always took, worrying a sentence or a line;
or come with protruded tongue to show
a silver stud;
or bamboozled by some guy who can't appreciate
the dragon tattooed on her breast, the filigree
around her thigh. This term she's done with school.

Four years she's siphoned every phrase,
or anecdote, or quote that's mine to dole.
She knows what I know,
or used to know, for in me sonnets fade.
Homer erodes
like sandstone worn by age.

Each year I grow emptier, more obsolete,
can barely grope
to words that once hung iridescent in my skull.
When, thirty years back, I asked my beloved tutor
how I'd ever pay him back, he said, *It's not
that linear. Only carry on this talk*

with someone else.
All his thoughts on Western Civ
would melt like ice without this kid—
hair dyed torch red, painted flames on her lug-sole boots.
She safety-pinned a plastic charm
of Our Lady's sacred heart to her sleeve.

Last night, to plot her destiny
she hurled at the world map a lopsided dart
and hit a South Seas flyspeck. Call collect,
I say, if you get stuck. Read
thus-and-such translation of Rilke *only.*
And though I sound like Polonius to myself,

she scribbles down my platitudes.
Without her like,
I'd live in the dull smear
of my own profession, each kid
a repeat, indistinct from the vanishing instants
that mark us made.

The hand that holds this pen's assembled by some force
newly manifest
in her face. She brought amazement for a spell,
then tore loose into the labyrinth I've meandered in
addled as a child, feeling along the string my teacher tied.
My eyes stare out from ever deeper sockets, edged in mesh.

I watch her cross the snow-swirled quad
backpacked in hunter plaid, bent like an old scholar,
moving with care across the slippery earth.
Snow is falling
over the quad, like rare pages
shredded and dispersed by wind,

that wild white filling every place we've stepped.

(for Betsy Hogan)

ENTERING THE KINGDOM

As the boy's bones lengthened,
and his head and heart enlarged,
his mother one day failed

to see herself in him.
He was a man then, radiating
the innate loneliness of men.

His expression was ever after
beyond her. When near sleep
his features eased towards childhood,

it was brief.
She could only squeeze
his broad shoulder. What could

she teach him
of loss, who now inflicted it
by entering the kingdom

of his own will?

DESCENDING THEOLOGY: THE GARDEN

We know he was a man because, once doomed,
    he begged for reprieve. See him
grieving on his rock under olive trees,
        his companions asleep
on the hard ground around him
        wrapped in old hides.
Not one stayed awake as he'd asked.
        That went through him like a sword.
He wished with all his being to stay
            but gave up
bargaining at the sky. He knew
        it was all mercy anyhow,
unearned as breath. The Father couldn't intervene,
        though that gaze was never
not rapt, a mantle around him. This
        was our doing, our death.
The dark prince had poured the vial of poison
    into the betrayer's ear,
and it was done. Around the oasis where Jesus wept,
        the cracked earth radiated out for miles.
In the green center, Jesus prayed for the pardon
        of Judas, who was approaching
with soldiers, glancing up—as Christ was—into
        the punctured sky till his neck bones
ached. Here is his tear-riven face come
        to press a kiss on his brother.

HURT HOSPITAL'S BEST SUICIDE JOKES

In unfolded aluminum chairs the color of shit
        and set in a circle as if to corral some emptiness
            in this church basement deep in the dirt,
                strangers sit and tell stories.
Case sipped wine in a hot tub. Janice
        threw back shots in a dive.
                Bob drew blinds to smoke blunts and ate nothing
                    but cake frosting bought by the case.
The first lady of someplace swiped her son's meds
        to stay slim. Craig burst through bank doors,
                machine gun in hand. John geezed heroin:
                    with a turkey baster, he says, *into a neck vein.*
A cop shoved Mark's face in the mud,
        put a shoe on his neck to cuff him and ask
                where his friends were. *I had friends,*
                he said, *think I'd be here?*
Zola once wrote that the road from the shrine
        at Lourdes was impressively littered
                with crutches and canes but he noted
                    not one wooden leg.
In the garage, with your face through a noose,
    ·   you kick out the ladder, but the green rope won't give,
                and when your wife clicks the garage switch and the door
                    tilts up, there you dangle on tiptoe.
Alive, all of us, on this island where we sip only
                black liquids or clear water and face down the void
                    we've shaped, and should our eyes meet
                        what howls erupt—like jackals we bawl
to find ourselves upright.

                                (for Patti Macmillan)

I opened up my shirt to show this man
the flaming heart he lit in me, and I was scooped up
like a lamb and carried to the dim warm.
I who should have been kneeling
was knelt to by one whose face
should be emblazoned on every coin and diadem:

no bare-chested boy, but Ulysses
with arms thick from the hard-hauled ropes.
He'd sailed past then clay gods
and the singing girls who might have made of him

a swine. That the world could arrive at me
with him in it, after so much longing—
impossible. He enters me and joy
sprouts from us as from a split seed.

THE FIRST STEP

From your first step toward me
        I sprang to life, though stood
                stock still. Our gazes locked.
You ambled up, I couldn't move.
        My swagger stopped.
              My breezy bravura
went windswept plain. I stood
        and let you come. For months we talked,
              but the chair you occupied sat
so far, you were an island oasis
        I couldn't reach. I barely heard the words
              your lush mouth shaped, just thirsted
for your breath to come
        easing down my lungs. Each time
              that mouth politely said goodnight
and turned so I could throw the bolt—
        upon that door, I'd softly bang my head.
              Until you asked (at last at
last) if you could browse my face,
        as if it were page or sacred tome.
              From then, the crosswalks told us *go,*
the maitre d's *right now.* From that first step,
        I had to stop the turning world
            to breathe you in,
and now some nights
        tend toward you whom
              I never was intended for.

(for Peter Straus)

A TAPESTRY FIGURE ESCAPES FOR OCCUPANCY
IN THE REAL WORLD, WHICH INCLUDES
THE DEATH OF HER MOTHER

You'd like the unseeable shuttle to stop
tocking off the ticked seconds
drawing tight strands of wind around you,

blue smoke, ether, wants. You'd like
the tapestry pattern to stop growing
around your minor figure.

Such a large green pasture already
and so much of which
you're not kept abreast, must only guess

from the trees' chord changes.
When you escape the tapestry and plop out,
you're on a street corner pondering left or right

when a loud whoosh from behind
whirls you around to find glowing
speed lines of some sudden absence.

Seraphim or incubus? Guardian or assassin?
Later, you slumber in the night boat
and wake feeling a neck-tug

like a noose or a shepherd's hook,
but it's only your own veined hands
trying to cut off that shriek

that got choked back
in childhood, but which now
boils up at certain instants like bile

Say the lover you're about to leave intones
a soliloquy on your hair. Say your mother's ashes
come in a Ziploc bag, on which you find writ

in some felt-tip, "Mom
one-half." You dip your right hand
in that gray flour, and its gravity

in your palm's scale is nothing. Love
is so rare, any such handful of ash
holds the whole world's weight.

unless, unless . . .
In your plunge through the gibbet door
the thread that darned you here

gets tied in a love knot and bitten free.

You were born inside barbed wire,
      black lines whose intervals of spiked stars
           were all you could steer by within
the vectors of that slaughterhouse. Poland otherwise starless.
      The stomp of jackboots down your block
           implanted the two-step iamb.
Then the sickle swung, a fine-honed moon
      at neck level, and the invaders' helmets toppled
           along with the listless or uncharged.
Many names in the gulag logbooks
      were printed in vanishing ink.
           You posed as scarecrow and birds
alit your arms. You posed as clerk, and no one
      was fooled. You went alone over a white steppe
           of snowy paper. Nightly your pen nib
traced the old gods' impotence.

      Here in the alleged first world,
           things cost a lot.
We suffer the luxury of disbelief,
      endure grim comfort. Our men are fat,
           our women spider thin.
Our scholars seek to cancel any history
      they find unsavory, or to untether words
           from referents till they sink
like sad balloons. Please send help.
      You may have crossed the checkpoint
           to the impalpable, but we hear across

those barricades what radar
        can't detect, nor censors blacken:
                your words, which pin our shoulders back,
drumbeats for the war that never passes.

                                    (for Zbigniew Herbert)

FOR A DYING TOMCAT WHO'S RELINQUISHED
HIS FORMER HISSING AND PREDATORY NATURE

I remember the long orange carp you once scooped
from the neighbor's pond, bounding beyond
her swung broom, across summer lawns

to lay the fish on my stoop. Thanks
for that. I'm not one to whom offerings
often get made. You let me feel

how Christ might when I kneel,
weeping in the dark
over the usual maladies: love and its lack.

Only in tears do I speak
directly to him and with such
conviction. And only once you grew frail

did you finally slacken into me,
dozing against my ribs like a child.
You gave up the predatory flinch

that snapped the necks of so many
birds and slow-moving rodents.
Now your once powerful jaw

is malformed by black malignancies.
It hurts to eat. So you surrender in the way
I pray for: Lord, before my own death,

let me learn from this animal's deep release
into my arms. Let me cease to fear
the embrace that seeks to still me.

COAT HANGER BENT INTO HALO

Gathering up my mother's clothes for the poor,
I find the coathanger that almost aborted me,
or so I dub it—the last hand clung to the high rod.
      Unwound, it could have poked

through the pink, puckered hole of her cervix
to spill me before I got going good.
Instead, from the furred litter of souls squirming
      to be visible, I was picked.

May I someday spy Mother's poppy-studded hat
on the skull of a street-corner gospel singer
swarming with sores. May I twist from this black wire
      a halo to crown my son's head.

LAST LOVE

For years I chose the man to suit the instant,
        from good guy to goat boy,
dreadlocked to crewcut. Not one could bridal me.
        In place of lace veil,
I peered from bandage gauze. And if,
        in rage, some suitor
tore that off, the red sun was a scald, and I felt
        scalped and rocket-shot
onto the nearest flight. So everyone I kissed
        left hurt. One man broke
the table I served him bread on. Another
        claimed my heart
was arsenic at its core. When my last love came,
        he slid a palm across
mine eyes, lent me his mouth
        (a bitten plum)
lay his head in the middle of me, bent me
        to that. Nights now,
my face rests on the meadow of his chest—
        so I'm a loose-petaled poppy
blown open, a girl again, for the first time
        hearing the earth's heartbeat.

THE ICE FISHERMAN

Because Grandpa Joe pronounced way
long ago, *They's fish*
big as Cadillacs down there, the ice fisherman
hacked a hole
and stood above a slush abyss
in steel-toed boots. Headphoned to the Pops—
engrossed, he couldn't hear the spider cracks.

When the river chasmed under him,
it was a blind
plunge into white flame, headphones
drifting down to silt. He rolled like a walrus,
body chub keeping him up
as green currents pulled him seaward at a tilt.
He felt the scarf his wife had knit an iron noose.

He failed to feel his hands.
His numb lips pressed to the river's spine, to suck
slid inches of air.
When he skimmed under the town rink,
music blurred and bored into his hurt ears.
Maybe some grappling hook wielded by solid citizens
would boost him, heave him

steaming onto the ice like a calved seal.
But the skaters' blades just cut scrollwork above his face.
Their blades went *whisk,* and he went out of reach.
Then out of his red mouth hole
he hollered up.

RED-CIRCLED WANT AD FOR MY SON
ON HIS COMMENCEMENT

The cabdriver wants a job where he can play
head-banging music loud, the director
to flicker forever on each skull's screen.

The scholar wants the whole oceanic mystery
to radiate from the next flipped page.
The drummer wants to keep time,

to beat it, the President to leave scorched
imprints of his oily dollar sign in every flaming
foreign field. I only want strafe bombers

to drop zillions of my books
over stadium and glen and rice
paddy, to satisfy the citizens who scream

for whatever streams from my Razorpoint,
plus for my son never to suffer
a knife tear in the frail

fabric of self, and to reckon
this loud, head-banging
world is a bequest no labor can earn.

SON'S ROOM

After my son left for college, come dusk,
I used to sit in his room painted green
like the first shoot of any plant,
caterpillar green, neon green of unripe papaya.
There was no stuffed polar bear to hold nor illustrated book
        whose valley I could wander down;

no laundry heap—no shirt an acre wide
I had to steam an iron across; no gunboat soccer shoes
to scrape mud off; no posters of beachball-breasted girls
urging him to sling on his backpack
and hop a train the length of Italy
        to the topless beach.

The walls were bare, the windows losing light.
If you've never been a kid, and choose to raise one, know
he'll wind up raising you. From whatever small drop
of care you start out with, he'll have to grow an ocean
and you a boat on which to sail from yourself
        forever, else you'll both drown.

From his desk, I'd stare across the courtyard
while night dragged its tide across the stones.
Once the fire escape vanished, I'd reenter the sarcophagus
my drinking boxed me in when he was a baby whose cry
ripped through the swathe of ether I hid in,
        and the certain, struggling

substance of him helped to my shoulder
did birth me to this flesh,
each luminous dawn
he grinned up and eventually down
to me from his towering height—each breath
        that filled him freed me

        from my own ribcage.

At the gold speckled counter, my pal in white apron—
index finger tapping his Arabic paper,
where the body count dwarfs
the one in my *Times*—announces,
You're killing my people.

But in Hell's Kitchen, even the Antichrist
ought to have coffee—one cream
and two sugars. *Blessings*
upon you, he says, and means it.

GARMENT DISTRICT SWEATSHOP

Through the plate glass, a vast concrete field of machines
repeating like war crosses on the Expressway
graveyard you pass coming in from the airport—so many.

You must be bred small
to fit such a slot.

Through the needle's eye a thread stabs
a slit void. You're on one side
then the other, where work gets done, gears engage.
Your wiry frame must bend like a fishhook
and hold there. Your black hair must convey restraint
with its ponytail or chopped bowl cut
or snake snarl at the nape.

That's at eyelevel, but below the hummingbird engines
of the work surface, the women dip into cool water.
It's a secret level where each woman
insists on using her free hand, where folded notes swim
clever as pilot fish—and white bottles of tablets
are passed—orange aspirin,
Extra Strength and Aleve.

By each woman a bag;
in each bag a billfold closes over a window
into another country's house—fat grandson,
rice-powdered daughter.

Some windows are vacant.
No one keeps the brothel's ceiling fan;
or the infant's mouth sewn shut.

On the factory floor all day, the tiny feet
are encased in embroidered shoes flimsy
as those you get buried in. They stomp down
on the machines' accelerators,
making the guises fit, never staying in one place.

OVERDUE PARDON FOR MOTHER WITH KNIFE

Some nights I startle up from sleep to gasp down
your death again like a draft of venom,
and feel I'm five, and see your flame-eyed shape

raise the knife you failed
to bury in my chest—whose gleam can still flash
across some desert in me, searing me awake.

I no longer curse that hand, as I once did,
but glorify the force that stayed it, set the blade
aside. Last week in the city you loved most

(the Paradise my birth stole you from),
I paused at a shop window
where spring heels floated

above staggered pedestals, as if tiptoeing
some drunken stair to the invisible.
Through the mist barrier,

your stare became a flicker
in the glass; then holding my face,
as if I were a gift, your hands (which grow now

on the ends of my own arms). It was me,
astonished, inside you.
Again in the chest, the heart's aperture (not

a dagger slot) opened. There
was the odd resolve I found in youth—
to guzzle down breath like sweet spirits,

as if a pillow just slid off my face.

From the far star points of his pinned extremities,
cold inched in—black ice and blood ink
till the hung flesh was empty. Lonely in that void
even for pain, he missed his splintered feet,
the human stare buried in his face.
He ached for two hands made of meat
he could reach to the end of.
In the corpse's core, the stone fist of his heart

began to bang on the stiff chest's door,
and breath spilled back into that battered shape. Now
it's your limbs he longs to flow into—
from the sunflower center in your chest
outward—as warm water
shatters at birth, rivering every way.

A BLESSING FROM MY SIXTEEN YEARS' SON

I have this son who assembled inside me
during Hurricane Gloria. In a flash, he appeared,
in a tiny blaze. Outside, pines toppled.

Phone lines snapped and hissed like cobras.
Inside, he was a raw pearl: microscopic, luminous.
Look at the muscled obelisk of him now

pawing through the icebox for more grapes.
Sixteen years and not a bone broken,
nor single stitch. By his age,

I was marked more ways, and small.
He's a slouching six-foot, three,
with implausible blue eyes, which settle

on the pages of Emerson's "Self-Reliance"
with profound belligerence.
A girl with a navel ring

could make his cell phone go *buzz,*
or an Afro'ed boy leaning on a mop at Taco Bell—
creatures strange to me as dragons or eels.

Balanced on a kitchen stool, each gives counsel
arcane as any oracle's. Rodney claims school
is harshing my mellow. Case longs to date

a tattooed girl, because he wants a woman
willing to do stuff she'll regret.
They've come to lead my son

into his broadening spiral.
Someday soon, the tether
will snap. I birthed my own mom

into oblivion. The night my son smashed
the car fender then rode home
in the rain-streaked cop car, he asked, *Did you*

and Dad screw up so much?
He'd let me tuck him in,
my grandmother's wedding quilt

from 1912 drawn to his goateed chin. *Don't*
blame us, I said. *You're your own*
idiot now. At which he grinned.

The cop said the girl in the crimped Chevy
took it hard. He'd found my son
awkwardly holding her in the canted headlights,

where he'd draped his own coat
over her shaking shoulders. *My fault,*
he'd confessed right off.

Nice kid, said the cop.

(for Dev Milburn)

ORPHANAGE

Now you've joined the mist specters we once
          peered into the night waves
to make out—the sparks from driftwood fire
          whooshing up the black sky,
smoke rings, mown grass, Shalimar, a handful
          of earth, turpentine, breath—they are
your substance now in the glorious,
          every fragrance, afterglow, aura,
and your face permanent marble as the final
          snapshot willed it.
And just as a child will cling to the creamiest
          silk slip helpless while it glides
from the grasp, so I sensed your soul shedding
          your hand, a lost glove
whose nonexistent heft I in memory keep
          holding though now you are
beyond us. No headlights will announce
          your arrival—high heels
waggling on gravel when you aimed
          that finger at the moon,
saying, *I have an earring like that.*

STILL MEMORY

The dream was so deep
the bed came unroped from its moorings,
drifted upstream till it found my old notch

in the house I grew up in,
then it locked in place.
A light in the hall—

my father in the doorway, not dead
just home from the graveyard shift
smelling of crude oil and solvent.

In the kitchen, Mother rummages through silver
while the boiled water poured
in the battered old drip pot

unleashes coffee's smoky odor.
Outside, the mimosa fronds, closed all night,
open their narrow valleys for dew.

Around us, the town is just growing animate,
its pulleys and levers set in motion.
My house starts to throb in the old hole.

My twelve-year-old sister steps fast
because the bathroom tiles
are cold and we have no heat other

than what our bodies can carry.
My parents are not yet born each
into a small urn of ash.

My ten-year-old hand reaches
for a pen to record it all
as would become long habit.

MEDITATIO

In the back's low hollow sometimes
a weightless hand guides me, gentle pressure
so I tack soft as a sailboat. *(Go there)*

Soften the space between your eyes (smudge
of eucalyptus), the third eye
opens. There's the wide vermilion sky

that cradled us before birth,
and the sun pours its golden sap
to preserve me like His precious insect.

FACING ALTARS: POETRY AND PRAYER

TO CONFESS MY UNLIKELY Catholicism in *Poetry*—the journal that first published some of the godless twentieth-century disillusionaries of J. Alfred Prufrock and his pals—feels like an act of perversion kinkier than any dildo-wielding dominatrix could manage on HBO's *Real Sex Extra.* I can't even blame it on my being a cradle Catholic, some brainwashed escapee of the pleated skirt and communion veil who—after a misspent youth and facing an Eleanor Rigby–like dotage—plodded back into the confession booth some rainy Saturday.

Not victim but volunteer, I converted in 1996 after a lifetime of undiluted agnosticism. Hearing about my baptism, a friend sent me a postcard that read, "Not you on the Pope's team. Say it ain't so!" Well, while probably not the late Pope's favorite Catholic (nor he my favorite Pope), I took the blessing and ate the broken bread. And just as I continue to live in America and vote despite my revulsion for many U.S. policies, I continue to take the sacraments despite my fervent aversion to certain doctrines. Call me a cafeteria Catholic if you like, but to that I'd say, Who isn't?

Perversely enough, the request for this essay showed up last winter during one of my lowest spiritual gullies. A blizzard's dive-bombing winds had kept all the bodegas locked for the second day running (thus depriving New Yorkers of newspapers and orange juice), and I found—in my otherwise bare mailbox—a letter asking me to write about my allegedly deep and abiding faith. That very morning, I'd confessed to my spiritual adviser that while I still believed in God, he had come to seem like Miles Davis, some nasty genius scowling out from under his hat, scornful of my mere being and on the verge of waving me off the stage for the crap job I was doing. The late William Matthews has a great line about Mingus, who "flurried" a musician from the stand by saying, "We've suffered a diminuendo in personnel. . . ." I felt doomed to be that diminuendo, an erasure mark that matched the erasure mark I saw in the grayed-out heavens.

In this state—what Dickinson called "sumptuous destitution"—prayer was a slow spin on a hot spit, but poetry could still draw me out of myself, easing my loneliness as it had since earliest kidhood. Poets were my first priests, and poetry itself my first altar. It was a lot of other firsts, too, of course: first classroom/chatroom/confessional. But it was most crucially the first source of awe for me, partly because of how it could ease my sense of isolation: it was a line thrown from seemingly glorious Others to my drear-minded self.

From a very early age, when I read a poem, it was as if the poet's burning taper touched some charred filament in my chest to light me up. The transformation could extend from me outward. Lifting my face from the page, I often faced my fellow creatures with less dread. Maybe buried in one of them was an ache or tenderness similar to the one I'd just been warmed by. Thus, poetry rarely failed to create for me some semblance of community, even if the poet reaching me was some poor wretch even more abject than myself. Poetry never left me stranded, and as an atheist most of my life, I presumed its comforts were a highbrow, intellectual version of what religion did for those more gullible believers in my midst—dumb bunnies to a one, the faithful seemed to me, till I became one.

In the Texas oil town where I grew up, I was an unfashionably bookish kid whose brain wattage was sapped by a consuming inner life others just didn't seem to bear the burden of. In a milieu where fierceness won fights, I was thin-skinned and hyper-vigilant. I just had more frames per second than other kids.

Plus, early on, I twigged to the fact that my clan differed from our neighbors. Partly because my atheist/artist mother painted nekked women and guzzled vodka straight out of the bottle, kids weren't allowed to enter my yard. She was seductive and mercurial and given to deep doldrums and mysterious vanishings, and I sought nothing so much as her favor. Poetry was my first conscious lure. Even as a preschooler, I could recite the works of cummings and A. A. Milne to draw her out of a sulk sometimes.

In my godless household, poems were the closest we came to sacred speech—the only prayers said. I remember Mother bringing me Eliot's poems from the library, and she not only swooned over them, she swooned over my swooning over them, which felt close as she came to swooning over me.

At age five—no doubt with my older sister's help—I was memorizing speeches from *Hamlet* and *Lear* and *Macbeth*. By the summer I was twelve, I'd developed a massive crush not only on the local lifeguard, but on J. Alfred Prufrock—a poem I learned in its entirety without comprehending much of. The suffocating alienation it evoked—even though set in bourgeois London long before my birth—resembled my own preadolescent inferno, but ennobled by Eliot's gorgeous language, exalted by that. Prufrock's jump-cut world, like mine, was also profane, starting with its seductive invitation to wander the grimy alleys under a cruelly anesthetized Heaven.

Where the locals saw in me an underfed misfit who wouldn't need a training bra for a long time, I knew old Prufrock would have fathomed the seventh-grade deeps in me and found me fetching. He wouldn't presume I was a suck-up if I knew how to spell Dostoevsky. He spoke of headless John the Baptist not with Bible Belt reverence but with irony, going so far as to super-impose his own head—going bald no less—on the platter where the saint's went! And since the hair on girls' arms could make Prufrock squeevy, he *understood* how the hairy legs of the life-guard both riveted and alarmed me as—all summer—I tried to look up the leg hole of his bathing suit. Prufrock sensed the skull under his own unlined face, the way I did. He was a young guy who felt old. Making J. Alfred's acquaintance, I learned that I was more than an egghead or a crybaby: I was by-God profound—a huge step up in junior-high self-concept, believe me.

Even my large-breasted and socially adroit older sister *got* Eliot—though Lecia warned me off telling kids at school that I read that kind of stuff. I remember sitting on our flowered bedspread reading Eliot to Lecia while she primped for a date. *Read it again, the whole thing.* She was a fourteen-year-old leaning into the mirror with a Maybelline wand, saying, *Goddamn, that's great. . . .*

Yet against her advice, I auditioned for my junior-high speech contest using "Prufrock," and the English teacher who headed the drama club sprinted down the auditorium aisle waving her hands before I got through as if I'd brought in a page from *Tropic of Cancer* to perform in G-string with pasties. (Longfellow's "Hiawatha" took its place, which, unfortunately, I can also still recite a good hunk of).

While my oil worker daddy, who never picked up a book in his life, might seem left out of this literary henhouse, in fact, Daddy also marveled at poems I picked for him—Frost mostly, and Kipling and Williams. (Later he'd particularly love the poems of Gwendolyn Brooks and Etheridge Knight). He was himself a black-belt barroom storyteller, master of comic idiom—repository for such poetic phrases as "it's raining like a cow pissing on a flat rock." His love of language made words his sacraments, too. Poetry was the family's religion. Beauty bonded us.

Church language works that way among believers, I would wager—whether prayer or hymn. Uttering the same noises in unison is part of what consolidates a congregation (along with shared rituals like baptisms and weddings, which are mostly words). Like poetry, prayer often begins in torment, until the intensity of language forges a shape worthy of both labels: "true" and "beautiful." (Only in my deepest prayers does language evaporate, and this wide and wordless silence takes over.)

But if you're in a frame of mind gloomy enough to refuse prayer, despite its having worked bona fide miracles for you before, nothing satisfies like a dark poem. Maybe wrestling with gnarly language occupies the loud and simian chatter of a dismayed mind, but for me the relief comes to some extent from a hookup to another creature. The compassion innate in having someone—however remote—verbalize your despair or lend a form to it can salve the jibbering psyche.

Last winter—my most recent spate of protracted bereavement—my faith got sandblasted away for more than a month. Part of this was due to circumstances. Right after I moved to New York, fortune delivered a triple whammy: my kid off to college, a live-in love ending brutally, then medical maladies kept me laid up for weeks alone. However right and proper each change was, I was left in a bleak and sleepless state—suddenly (it felt sudden, as if a magician's silk kerchief covered the world in an eye blink) God seemed vaporous as any perfume.

To kneel and pray in this state is almost physically painful. At best, it's like talking into a bucket. At worst, you feel like a chump, some heartsick fool still pasting up valentines for a long-gone cad. Bowing my head, I could almost hear my every entreaty whispered back in a snide voice. Maybe a few times I dipped into the darker Psalms or the Book of Job. But more often I let "the terrible sonnets" of Gerard Manley Hopkins shape my desolation,

I am gall. I am heartburn. God's most deep decree
Bitter would have me taste: my taste was me.
Bones built in me, flash filled, blood brimmed the curse.
Selfyeast of spirit a dull dough sours. I see
The lost are like this, and their scourge to be
as I am mine, their sweating selves; but worse.

I was also reading that bleak scribbler Bill Knott, who's a great companion for the sipping of gall. He'd aptly captured my spiritual state in "Brighton Rock by Graham Greene," where he imagined a sequel for Greene's book: the ill-gotten child whom a criminal sociopath (Pinky Brown) conceived in the body of pitiful Rose Wilson before he died becomes a teenager in a skiffle band called Brighton Rockers, and the whole family's miserable existence resounds in the grotesque Mass mother Rose sits through.

Every Sunday now in church Rose slices

her ring finger off, onto the collection plate;
once the sextons have gathered enough
bodily parts from the congregation, enough

to add up to an entire being, the priest substitutes that entire being for the one
on the cross: they bring Him down in the name

of brown and rose and pink, sadness
and shame. His body, remade, is yelled at
and made to get a haircut, go to school,

study, to do each day like the rest
of us crawling through this igloo of hell
and laugh it up, show pain a good time,

and read Brighton Rock by Graham Greene.

This winter, I felt yelled at by the world at large and God in par-
ticular. The rhythm of Knott's final sentence says it all—"to DO
each DAY like the REST of us/. . . ."—the first phrase is a stair
plod, with an extra stumble step to line's end, where it becomes
a pratfall you take into slithering submission (no REST here)—
"CRAWling through this IGloo of HELL."

People usually (always?) come to church as to prayer and
poetry—through suffering and terror, need and fear—flaming
arrows gone thump in the heart. In some Edenic past, our ances-
tors began to evolve hardwiring that drives us (so I believe) to
make a noise beautiful enough to lay on the altar of the Creator/
Rain God/Fertility Queen. With both prayer and poetry, we use
elegance to exalt, but we also beg and grieve and tremble. We
suffer with prayer and poetry alike. Boy, do we suffer.

The would-be believers who sometimes ask me for help
with prayer (still a comic notion) often say it seems hypocritical
to turn to God only now during whatever crisis is forcing them
toward it—kid with leukemia, say, husband lost in the World

Trade Center. But no one I know has ever turned to God any other way. As the adage says, there are no atheists in foxholes (though reason suggests there are probably a couple). Maybe saints turn to God to exalt him, from innate righteousness. The rest of us tend to show up holding out a tin cup. Put the penny of your prayer in this slot and pull the handle—not an unusual approach. The Catholic church I attended in Syracuse, New York (St. Lucy's), said it best on the banner stretched across its front: SINNERS WELCOME.

That's how—nearly fifteen years back—I came to prayer, fleeing what James Laughlin (via *Pilgrim's Progress*) used to call the Slough of Despond, and over the years, prayer led me to God, and God led me to church—a journey fueled by some massively freakish coincidences, which proved over the years that any energy I spent seeking God paid off a hundredfold. It's a time-honored formula: I prayed, and my life got better, exponentially so. Otherwise, I'm not anywhere near virtuous enough to bother.

Okay, I couldn't stop drinking. I'd tried everything *but* prayer. And somebody suggested to me that I kneel every morning and ask God for help not picking up a cocktail, then kneel at night to say thanks. "But I don't believe in God," I said. Again Bill Knott came to mind:

People who get down
on their knees to me
are the answers to my prayers.

The very idea of prostrating myself brought up the old Marxist saw about religion being the opiate for the masses. God as a dictator forcing me to grovel? I wouldn't have it. One spiritual adviser at the time was an ex–heroin addict who radiated vigor. Janice had enough street cred for me to say to her, "Fuck that god. Any god who'd want people kneeling and sniveling—"

Janice cut me off. "You don't do it for God, you asshole," she said. She told me to try it like an experiment: Pray for thirty days, and see if I stayed sober and things looked up.

Franz Wright states my starting point nicely in "Request," here in its entirety from *The Beforelife:*

Please love me
and I will play for you
this poem
upon a guitar I made
out of cardboard and black threads
when I was ten years old.
Love me or else.

I started kneeling to pray morning and night—spitefully at first, in a bitter pout. The truth is, I still very much fancied the idea that glugging down Jack Daniel's would stay my turmoil, even though doing so had resulted in my driving into stuff with more molecular density than I. But I had an illiterate baby to whom many vows had been made, and—whatever whiskey's virtues—it had gotten hard to maintain my initial argument that drinking made me a calmer mom to a colicky infant. Whiskey was killing me, which—in those early days when I was jonesing for a drink—didn't seem such a bad idea for either my kid or me, given my ugly disposition.

Ergo, I prayed—not with the misty-eyed glee I'd seen on *Song of Bernadette,* nor with the butch conviction of Charlton Heston playing Moses in *Ten Commandments.* I prayed with belligerence, at least once with a middle finger aimed at the light fixture—my own small unloaded bazooka pointed at the Almighty. I said *Keep me sober,* in the morning. I said, *Thanks,* at night.

And though I'd been bouncing on and off the wagon for a few years, unable to give up booze for more than a period of weeks (with and without the help of other human beings), I didn't pick up a drink. Which seemed—to one who'd studied positivism and philosophy of science in college—a psychological payoff to the dumb process of getting on my knees twice a day to talk to myself. One MIT-trained scientist told me she prayed to her "sober self"— a palatable concept for the agnostic I was.

Poet Thomas Lux was one ex-drinker I saw a lot in Cambridge back then, since our babies were a year apart in age, and we'd often shove them through malls in their strollers or strap them to our bodies and nose around Louisa Solano's Grolier Poetry Book Shop.

Lux's first collection written without booze, *Half-Promised Land,* chronicled split worlds of Manichean dark and saving light. Later, in an interview for *Ploughshares,* I'd asked him how he'd quit drinking. His droll reply? "I drank one day. Then I didn't drink the next day, and I haven't had a drink since." His verses about salvation always came peppered with grotesque or forlorn figures. In "Tarantulas on a Life Buoy," the speaker vacationing in the tropics finds a bunch of spiders on a swimming-pool float.

> They usually drown—but
> if you want their favor,
> if you believe in justice,
> a reward for not loving
>
> the death of the ugly
> and even dangerous (the eel, hog snake,
> rats) creatures, if
>
> you believe these things, then
> you would leave a lifebuoy
> or two in your swimming pool at night.
>
> And in the morning
> you would haul ashore
> the huddled, hairy survivors

and escort them
back to the bush, and know
be assured that at least these saved,
as individuals would not turn up

again someday
in your hat, drawer,
or the tangled underworld
of your socks. . . .

This is old-fashioned secular humanism, kindness as social necessity. We should be nice to the menacing gang of kids on the subway so they don't stab us with ice picks at the next stop. But in one poem about his wife's car colliding with a moose ("Wife Hits Moose"), the poet thanks a "Supreme Intelligence" for his wife's survival.

Lux had truck with a Supreme Intelligence? That dismal bastard? The guy who'd once said of himself, grimly, "I'm no Richard Simmons" (referring to television's chubby cheerleader–cum–exercise sage for the elderly and overweight)?

One day when Lux was barbequing by a swimming pool for a gaggle of poets (Allen Grossman in a three-piece suit and watch fob comes to mind, God love him), I confessed to him I was mouthing daily prayers trying to maintain what Berryman might have called my *baffling odd sobriety.* The scene comes back to me with Lux poking at meat splayed on the grill while I swirled my naked son around the swimming pool. Did he actually *pray?* I couldn't imagine it—for Lux was a dark sucker.

Ever taciturn, Lux told me: I say thanks.

For what? I wanted to know. Robert Hass's *Praise* was a cult favorite at the time. He'd been the teacher in grad school who read Pound and Eliot and Stevens with me one enraptured semester. But Hass's own ardor for trees and birds and the coast—his penchant for worship—mystified me, because my poetic enterprise entailed our collective hurtle towards death (the prospect of my own death seeming specially tragic and unsung). For me, everything was too much, and nothing was enough.

My sidewinding nihilism was a predictable stance for a poet at the time. Even Hass's book was riddled with the disappointments deliverable by beauty or sex or marriage. In the 1980s, most of us could quote his lines: "All the new thinking is about loss./ In this, it resembles all the old thinking." (A sentence a pal and I used to warp by substituting "drinking" for "thinking"). The epigraph for *Praise* had a man facing down a huge and ominous monster and saying—from futility and blind fear—"I think I shall praise it." In a twisted cosmology I'd never articulated to myself back then, Hass's monster was God.

Back in Lux's pool, I honestly couldn't think of anything to be grateful for. I told Lux something like I was glad I still had all my limbs. That's what I mean about how my mind didn't take in reality before I began to practice some regular devotions.

I couldn't register the privilege of holding my blond and ring-leted boy, who chortled and bubbled and splashed on my lap.

It was a clear day, and Lux was standing in his surfer baggies at the barbeque turning sausages and chicken with one of those diabolical looking forks. In the considerable smoke, he looked like a bronzed Satan at the devil's cauldron he'd write about two decades later.

Say thanks for the sky, Lux said, say it to the floorboards. This isn't hard, Mare.

At some point, I also said to him, What kind of god would permit the Holocaust?

To which Lux said, You're not in the Holocaust.

In other words, what is the Holocaust my business?

No one ever had an odder guru than Thomas Lux, master of the Eeyore-esque, chronicler of the miseries that plague the working poor, but I started following his advice by mouthing rote thank-you's to the air, and right off, I discovered something. There was an entire aspect to my life that I had been blind to—the small, good things that came in abundance. A friend had once told me regarding his own faith, "I've memorized the bad news." So it seemed to me that my über-realistic worldview (we die, worms eat us, there is no God), to which I'd clung so desperately for its rationality, was never chosen for its basis in truth, nor for its efficacy in running my life. It was just a focal point around which my own tortured inwardness could twist.

Back when I was still shod in patent leather Mary Janes, my

mother had introduced me to despondency, spouting Nietzsche and Sartre, and she often sketched for my future—anybody's future—lonely travails across a landscape so perilous no one could traverse it unscarred.

Having, all my life disdained as nonsense any spiritual or religious practice, I eventually realized that I'd always believed in a magical force for evil. Like Hawthorne's minister in *The Black Veil,* I interpreted the world through my own grief or self-absorbed fear. My evocation of Holocaust victims had little to do with either my compassion for said victims or political fervor. It was part of the pinched worry about my own death, my own losses. If I didn't get a parking space, it was ever hateful Fate that steered the Alfa Romeo into it before me. Such was my *realistic* worldview.

Within a year of my talk with Lux, in a time of crisis (the end of my marriage), someone gave me a prayer allegedly from St. Francis of Assisi—one of those rote prayers that cradle Catholics resent having drilled into them, and I started saying it with my five-year-old son every night:

Lord, make me an instrument of Thy peace.
Where there is hatred, let me sow love;
where there is conflict, pardon;
where there is doubt, faith;
where there is despair, hope;
where there is sadness, joy;
where there is darkness, light.

they limited techniques for the great truth
that they showed, that we're made in the image
of each other and don't know it.

"The Generations," *Time and Money*

So the exercises during Mass that may rankle a lapsed Catholic as "empty rituals" made me feel like part of a tribe, in a way, and the effect carried over in me even after church.

Poetry had consoled me in the same way, with Eucharistic qualities that Hass had first pointed out. In memorizing the poems I loved, I "ate" them in a way. I breathed as the poet breathed to recite the words: Someone else's suffering and passion entered my body to change me, partly by joining me to others in a saving circle.

Prayer had been one cornerstone of my altar, but only after a lifetime of poetry had propped me up. In language, I'd always found a way out of myself—first to my mother, then to a wider community (the poets I first imagined, then later sometimes got to meet), then to a poetry audience for which I wrote, then to the Lord, who (paradoxically) speaks most powerfully to me through quiet. People will think I'm nuts when I say I prayed about whether to take a job or to end my marriage or to switch my son's school. I prayed about what to write and wrote a bestseller that dug me out of my single mom's financial hole.

Don't let me brag too much. I also pray to write like Wallace

Stevens and don't. I pray to be five-ten and remain five inches short. Doubt still plagues me. As Zola once noted vis-á-vis his trip back from Lourdes, he saw crutches and wheelchairs thrown out but not artificial legs.

Milosz is more articulate about it in "Veni Creator":

I am only a man: I need visible signs.
I tire easily, building the stairway of abstraction.
Many a time I asked, you know it well, that the statue in
    church
lift its hand, only once, just once, for me. . . .

Prayer has yielded comfort and direction—all well and good. But imagine my horror when I began to have experiences of joy.

"You were not meant for pleasure, you were meant for joy," Thomas Merton wrote. I'm still a great acolyte of pleasure—the perfect plate of stinging-nettle tagliatelle; the taxicab kiss; the oiled heel of the masseur's hand sloping off my lower back, leaving a wake of release. For me, joy arrives in the body (where else would it find us?), yet doesn't originate there. Nature never drew me into joy as it does others, but my fellow creatures (God's crown of creation) often spark joy in me: kids on a Little League diamond in full summer—even idly tossing their mitts into the air; the visual burst of a painted Basquiat angel in Everlast boxing shorts at the Brooklyn Museum last week (can't stop thinking about it).

Add love of someone into the interaction, and the transformation has the weight of animal history behind it. My seventeen years' son at night in a winter blizzard buries our kitten in a shoebox so I don't have to see her run over—his snow-flushed face later breaking the news to me—my grief countered by radical joy at his kindness.

In the right mind-set, the faces that come at me on the New York street are like Pound's apparitions, "petals on a wet, black bough." For me, joy always involves breaking out of myself toward someone else. Every year my students lend me sufficient awe to let me fall in love with poetry as if for the first time. Only empathy wakes me from the plodding doldrums I'm inclined to. There's always joy in seeing how others see, even when it also entails a stab of pain. I'm thinking of the dude who sometimes sleeps in my doorway wearing a Hefty garbage bag tied around his neck— like a superhero's cape! *Excuse me,* he says, carefully rearranging himself as I step over him. My admiration for this courtliness brings an odd joy with it.

But nothing can maim a poet's practice like joy. As Henry de Montherlant noted, "Happiness writes white." Few poets— in this century or any other—have founded an opus on joy. We can all drum up a few ecstatic poems here and there, but poetry has often spread the virus of morbidity. It's been shared comfort for the dispossessed. Yes, we have Whitman opening his arms to "the blab of the pave." We have James Wright breaking into blossom, but he has to step out of his body to do so. We have the revelatory moments of Tranströmer and the guilty pleasure and religious striving of Milosz. W.H. Auden captured the ethos when he wrote, "The purpose of poetry is disenchantment." Poetry in the recent past hasn't allowed us much joy.

My own efforts to lighten this otherwise dour new collection seem pale. The poems about Christ salted through the book spend way more time on crucifixion than resurrection. I've written elegies galore, love poems bitter as those of Catullus. I've written from scorched-earth terror, and longing out the wazoo. My new aesthetic struggle is to accommodate joy as part of my literary enterprise, but I still tend to be a gloomy and serotonin-challenged bitch.

Shortly after the attacks on 9/11, I was asked to read for *The New Yorker*'s benefit and struggled with whether or not to include Holocaust survivor Paul Celan's agonized poem about the digging in mass graves. It moved from heavy resignation to fury at a God whose universe contained the graves' possibility:

> There was earth inside them, and
> they dug.
>
> They dug and they dug, so their day
> went by for them, their night.
> And they did not praise God, who, so they heard,
>   wanted all this,
> who, so they heard, knew all this.

They dug and heard nothing more;
thcy did not grow wise, invented no song,
thought up for themselves no language.
They dug.

(translated from German by Michael Hamburger)

The cadence of the poem drummed out the relentless dirge of a people's grief, but was it perhaps too dark? The digging at Ground Zero was only blocks away, and perhaps the poem would fall on the audience like another blow. Celan wound up a suicide, after all.

A pal ultimately convinced me to read it. He reminded me that its conclusion suggests not just digging toward the lost, but also a collective digging into history, how one person in despair and loneliness digs toward the salvation of someone else—even if the other is only saved through memory. The poem concludes with a moment of awakening, the sound of a ring striking metal as one human being reaches another. Celan shifts his longing to a bittersweet nursery rhyme cadence that follows the German: *O einer, o keiner, o niemand, o du.*

On one, o none, o no one, o you:
Where did the way lead when it led nowhere?
you dig, and I dig, and I dig towards you,
and on our finger the ring awakes.

Poetry and prayer alike offer such instantaneous connection—one person groping from a dark place to meet with another in an instant that strikes fire. It's a ring that's struck on "our finger" (actually it looks like "the finger" in the German)—everyone's finger. We are married to each other, even in (especially in?) death, the poem tells us.

Rewind to last winter: my spiritual wasteland, when I received a request from *Poetry* to write about my faith. It was the third such request I'd gotten in a little more than a week, and it came from an editor I felt I owed in some ways. How many times did Peter deny knowing Christ?

I know, I know, my skeptical reader. It's only my naive faith that makes such a simple request (times three) seem like a tap on the shoulder from the Almighty, but for one whose experience of joy has come in middle age on the rent and tattered wings of depression and disbelief, it suffices. Having devoted the first half of my life to the dark, I feel obliged to locate any pinpoint of light now. And writing this essay did fling open a window so some column of sun shone down on me again. When I hit my knees again during Lent, I felt God's sturdy presence, and I knew right off it wasn't God who'd checked out in the first place.

Milosz, who dubbed himself the "least normal person in Father Chomski's class," describes the sense of alert presence prayer can yield in "Late Ripeness"—a lit-up poem of the type I aspire to write:

Not soon, as late as the approach of my ninetieth year
I felt a door opening in me and I entered
the clarity of early morning.

One after another my former lives were departing
like ships together with their sorrow.
And the countries, cities, gardens, the bays of seas
assigned to my brush came closer,
ready now to be described better than before.

I was not separated from people, grief and pity joined us.
We forget—I kept saying—that we are all children of
    the King. . . .

That's why I pray and poetize: to be able to see my brothers and
sisters despite my own (often petty) agonies, to partake of the
majesty that's every sinner's birthright.

HELL'S KITCHEN
JULY 2005